COUNTRY AND SUBURBAN HOUSES OF THE TWENTIES

WITH PHOTOGRAPHS AND FLOOR PLANS

Edited by

Bernard Wells Close

DOVER PUBLICATIONS, INC.
Mineola, New York

Bibliographical Note

This Dover edition, first published in 2004, is an unabridged republication of the work originally published in 1922 by the Architectural Book Publishing Co., New York, under the title *American Country Houses of Today: Small Houses, Bungalows, Etc.* The only significant alteration consists in moving the frontispiece from its original position inside the book to the inside front cover.

Library of Congress Cataloging-in-Publication Data

American country houses of today.
    Country and suburban houses of the twenties : with photographs and floor plans / edited by Bernard Wells Close.
        p. cm.
    Originally published: American country houses of today. New York : Architectural Book Pub. Co., 1922.
    ISBN 0-486-43631-4 (pbk.)
    1. Country homes—United States—Designs and plans. 2. Suburban homes—United States—Designs and plans. 3. Architecture—United States—20th century—Designs and plans. I. Close, Bernard Wells. II. Title.

NA7561.A67 2004
728'.37'097309042—dc22

                                                                2004055108

Manufactured in the United States of America
Dover Publications, Inc., 31 East 2nd Street, Mineola, N.Y. 11501

Beauty, convenience, grandeur of thought and quaint expression are as near to us as to any, and if the American artist will study with hope and love the precise thing to be done by him, considering the climate, the soil, the length of the day and the wants of the people, he will create a house in which all these will find themselves fitted, and taste and sentiment will be satisfied also. —Emerson.

PREFACE

HERE are eighty country homes selected from the best available work recently done. Some of the authors specialize in country homes, some have made their reputation mainly upon them, and all have given much study to this most interesting branch of architectural practice.

Eighty families in their hundred differing ways, have met their problems as you strive to meet yours, that is in houses which are convenient in plan, expressive of what houses should say, and so designed that they may always be understood. If a house meets these conditions it is a good house.

For a house talks. Oh, indeed it does—it talks of grace, honesty, hospitality; or of shallow pretense and—but we're not talking of that kind of house. And if the next generation and the next shall say: "Yes, you are graceful, you are honest, you are hospitable," then it has been beyond peradventure a well-designed house.

These houses are not meant to copy but to help you to get a house of your own which shall be better for you than any of them. Some are very modest in size, some are larger, but let not the man of more limited means therefore turn away, for his wife will tell him

"Let me live in a house by the side of the road where the race of men go by."
                                                              —Foss.

that shopping is the art of examining things more expensive than she can pay for, in order to judge more intelligently of those she will finally buy.

Even a short life bears witness to the great progress in American domestic architecture. We well know that the period of our early buildings by craftsman-architects gave place to dearth of taste both in the supply and the demand. We have awaked from that. In the process of awakening we have had some bad dreams, crude copyings, exotic styles, but now a goodly and increasing number of architects are working in the spirit of true design, which means that you may readily get a house which, in spite of ever advancing standards, will remain a good house. If it does not achieve the monumental quality of perpetual youth, it should certainly have a respectable and respected old age. It is not always necessary that a house should conform to the traditions of the locality: precedents are but tools, not masters. True, one would not choose to place a house of sharp vertical lines and towers on a treeless plateau, or one of "the style of the western plains" in a prim New England elm-bordered street, but between these extremes there is much liberty. The question of form, and fitness to surrounding landscape, is more important than the recalling of past history.

The scope of this preface does not permit detailed discussion of the designing of a house:

To one who has been long in city pent,
'Tis very sweet to look into the fair
And open face of heaven — to breathe a prayer
Full in the smile of the blue firmament.
                                        —Keats.

the questions of view both of and from; the approach; the rising of
the sun and the going down thereof; materials;—all such matters
belong to the first consultations with the architect, before the house
is really designed at all, or rather their general settlement forms the
basis for the plan and the design.

Let us speak, therefore, of the human relationship to be established,
to the end that you as owner shall proceed hand in hand with some
sympathetic and knowledgeable person called the architect to the
completion of your house.

There are several ways to choose an architect, some are worse
than others. A poor way is this: to ask or allow two or more men,
usually totally unknown to the owner to submit free schemes for
the house. Happily this method is now less favored on both sides.
I have wondered how anyone expects his work to be attended to
by a man who is making these wild dashes after the next jobs. Almost
any other way will do to get track of an architect in the first place,
by seeing his work, actually or published, recommendations of
friends, etc. But after that, people go about it too shyly: they seem
to be as hesitant about talking to an architect whom they may not
finally employ, as one would be about proposing to a girl he did
not wish to marry. Do not hesitate to call on an architect and talk
things over, see if he seems to understand you, and appears to be
such a person as you can comfortably travel with along the important
road of house-building. Talk with his clients; of course he will

probably only mention those who are pleased, but you can at least see if they are people of discernment.

Remember the work of one who specializes in country homes is about as personal as that of the family doctor; you expect him to work with all his skill in your interest, and so he ought, therefore give him your first confidence carefully, then whole-heartedly, and pay him cheerfully, to the end that when you sit together by your new and well-drawing fireplace, the architect may hear some such sweet words as these: "Well, Jones, we've had a good time building this house together. I'm almost sorry it's over, but if I were doing it again I'd do just the same."

Three people say "I built this house"—the builder, the owner, the architect. In the sense we are speaking of the last two build the house. The only successful house is built by these two working together, each ready to concede the other's praise.

Now as to the use of this book. After you have glanced at an exterior view examine the plan, as the plan was, or should have been, the starting point. You will then be able to understand the outside better and be able to judge whether that house holds any suggestion for you. If you find no house you would exactly repeat so much the better, for no house belongs in any other place, and no one has a right to repeat another man's house. In fact a very intelligent

"He lives to build, not boast, a glorious race."

choice of an architect is sometimes expressed like this: "I saw my friend Smith's house which you did; there isn't much about it I like for myself, for my site and general wants are quite different, but you dealt with him logically and satisfactorily, so I think the same methods would get me the house I want." You have a perfect right to expect of your architect the best house he has ever done. That will be a pretty good test of his ability to make a house out of a given set of requirements and a personality.

In general, you will see in this book a series of houses which represents what many others have done before you in achieving their homes, some compromises probably of desires with bank accounts, some real friendships formed in the doing, and none we trust broken, houses which are adjudged good architecture, and which may help you finally to establish strong roots of domestic tranquillity.

ALFRED BUSSELLE.

RESIDENCE OF MR. ELLIS BROWN, JR., DOWNINGTON, PA.

MELLOR, MEIGS AND HOWE, ARCHITECTS, PHILADELPHIA, PA.

1

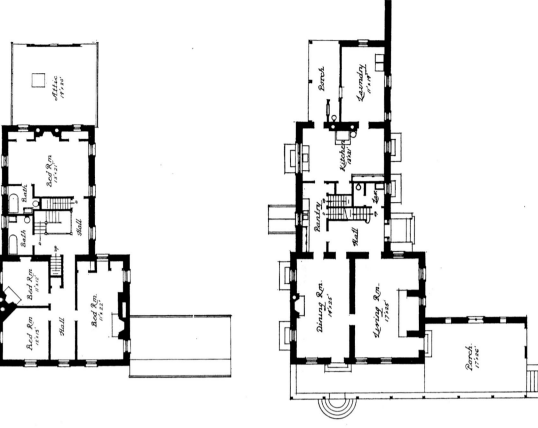

FRONT DOOR—RESIDENCE OF ELLIS G. BROWN, JR., DOWNINGTON, PA.

MELLOR, MEIGS AND HOWE, ARCHITECTS, PHILADELPHIA, PA.

RESIDENCE OF MR. GEORGE WASHURST, ARCHITECT, PHILIPSE MANOR, N. Y.

COUNTRY AND SUBURBAN HOUSES OF THE TWENTIES

RESIDENCE OF MR. GEORGE WASHURST, ARCHITECT, PHILIPSE MANOR, N. Y.

4

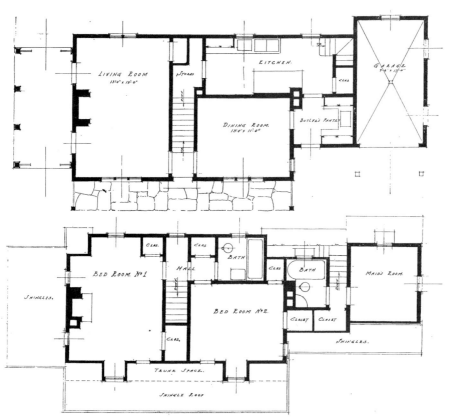

HOUSE OF MRS. M. H. FALLON, PIERMONT, N. Y.

AYMAR EMBURY II, ARCHITECT, NEW YORK

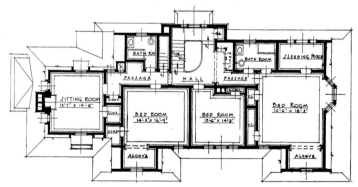

· PLAN · OF · SECOND · FLOOR ·

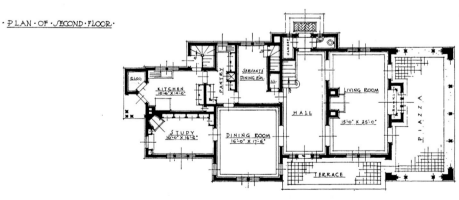

· PLAN · OF · FIRST · FLOOR ·

RESIDENCE FOR MRS. L. W. DODD, NEW HAVEN, CONN.

AYMAR EMBURY II, ARCHITECT, NEW YORK

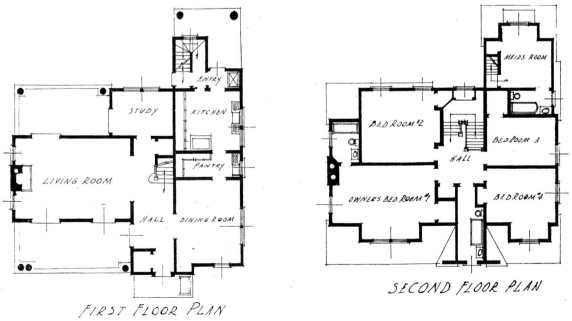

FIRST FLOOR PLAN

SECOND FLOOR PLAN

RESIDENCE OF MR. CHARLES MULLALY AT PHILIPSE MANOR, N. Y.

DWIGHT JAMES BAUM, ARCHITECT, NEW YORK

HOUSE FOR MRS. THOMAS D. HOPPER, RYE, N. Y.

LEWIS COLT ALBRO, ARCHITECT, NEW YORK

8

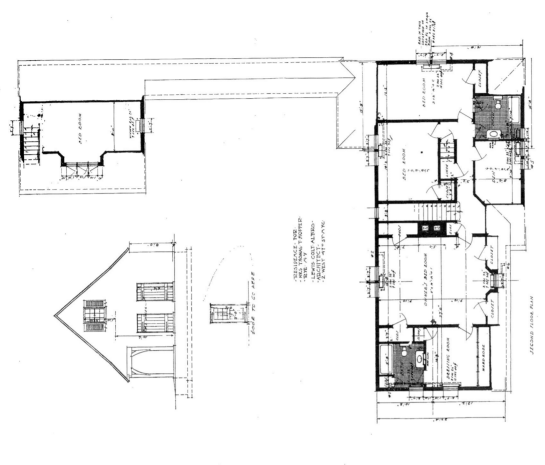

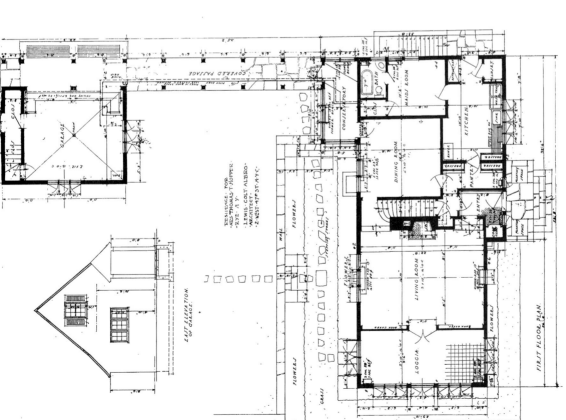

HOPPER RESIDENCE, RYE, N. Y.

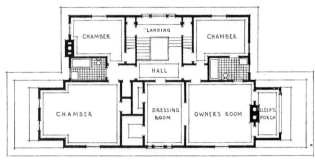

SECOND FLOOR PLAN

FIRST FLOOR PLAN

RESIDENCE OF MR. FRANK M. SIMPSON, LITTLE FALLS, N. Y.

DWIGHT JAMES BAUM, ARCHITECT, NEW YORK

10

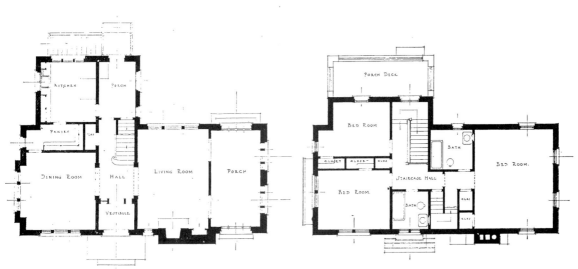

HOUSE AT FOREST HILLS, L. I.

SAGE FOUNDATION HOMES CO., ARCHITECTS, NEW YORK

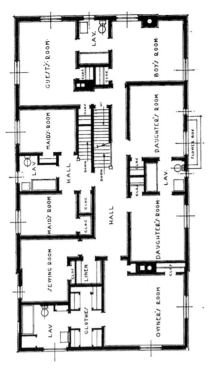

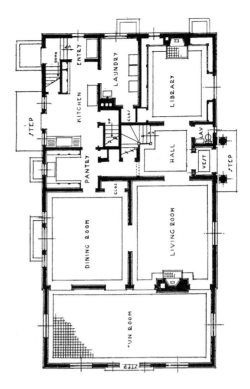

RESIDENCE OF JUDGE NASH ROCKWOOD AT RIVERDALE-ON-HUDSON, N. Y. C.

DWIGHT JAMES BAUM, ARCHITECT, NEW YORK

12

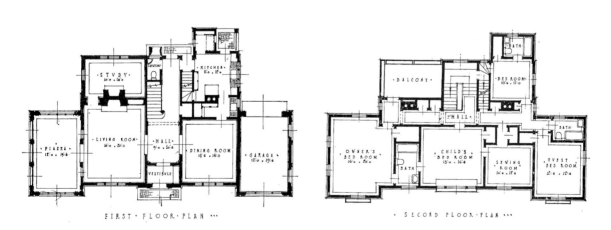

FIRST · FLOOR · PLAN ···   · SECOND · FLOOR · PLAN ···

RESIDENCE FOR MR. JOSEPH E. BUSH, FIELDSTON, N. Y.
DWIGHT JAMES BAUM, ARCHITECT, NEW YORK

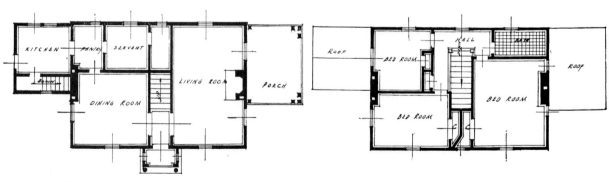

· FIRST · FLOOR · PLAN ·
· Scale · 1/8" · 1'- 0"

· SECOND · FLOOR · PLAN ·
Scale 1/8" = 1'- 0"

HOUSE AT LARCHMONT GARDENS, N. Y.

PHELPS BARNUM, ARCHITECT, NEW YORK

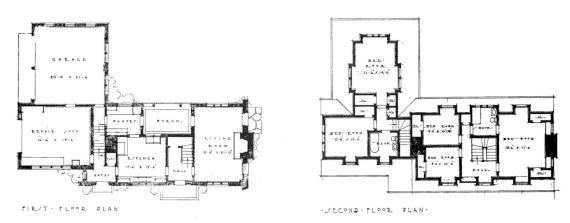

HOUSE FOR EDWIN THANHOUSER, ESQ., OYSTER BAY

TOOKER AND MARSH, ARCHITECTS, NEW YORK

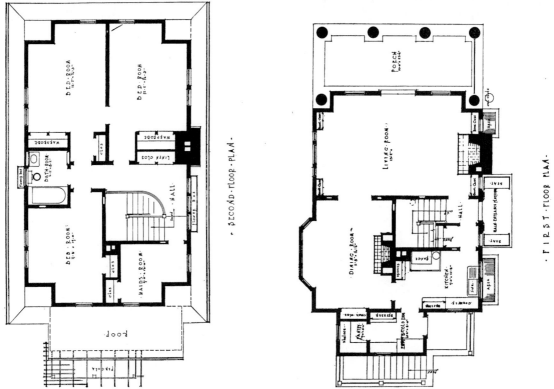

HOUSE FOR MR. AMOS D. CARVER, LOCUST VALLEY, L. I.

TOOKER AND MARSH, ARCHITECTS, NEW YORK

FIRST FLOOR PLAN   SECOND FLOOR PLAN

RESIDENCE OF MR. FRED SMITH, ARCHITECT, AT BALDWIN, L. I.

DETAIL RESIDENCE OF FRED SMITH, ARCHITECT, BALDWIN, L. I.

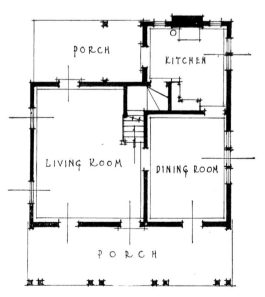

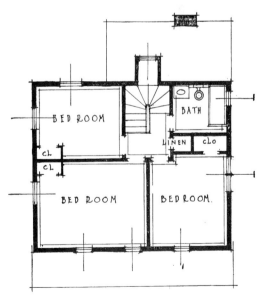

FIRST FLOOR PLAN   SECOND FLOOR PLAN.

RESIDENCE AT BALDWIN, L. I.

FRED SMITH, ARCHITECT, BALDWIN, L. I.

19

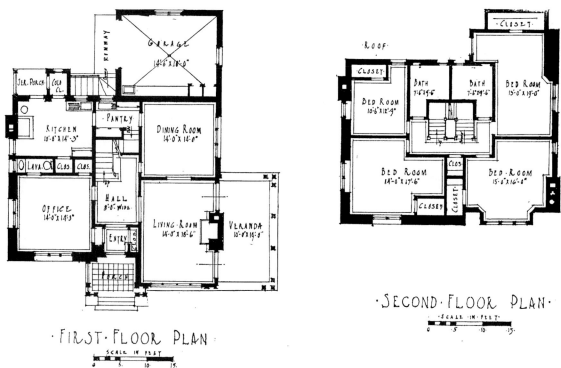

· FIRST · FLOOR · PLAN ·

· SECOND · FLOOR · PLAN ·

RESIDENCE FOR DR. HEATON, FIELDSTON, N. Y.

MANN AND MacNEILL, ARCHITECTS, NEW YORK

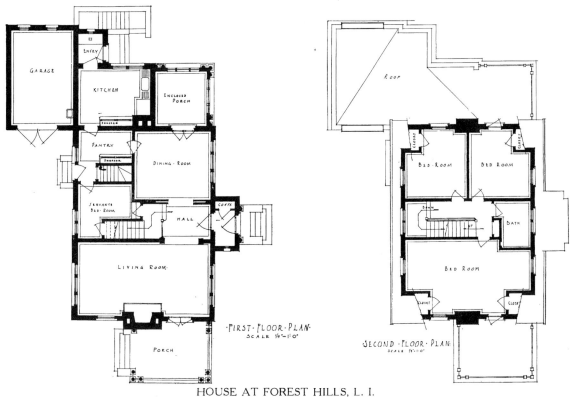

·FIRST·FLOOR·PLAN·
SCALE ¼"=1'0"

·SECOND·FLOOR·PLAN·
SCALE ¼"=1'0"

HOUSE AT FOREST HILLS, L. I.

SAGE FOUNDATION CO., ARCHITECTS, NEW YORK

21

RESIDENCE OF B. F. WINCHELL, JR., FIELDSTON ROAD, UPPER N. Y. C.

DWIGHT JAMES BAUM, ARCHITECT, NEW YORK

22

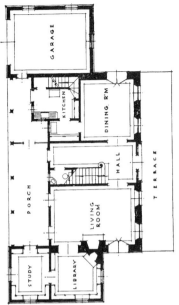

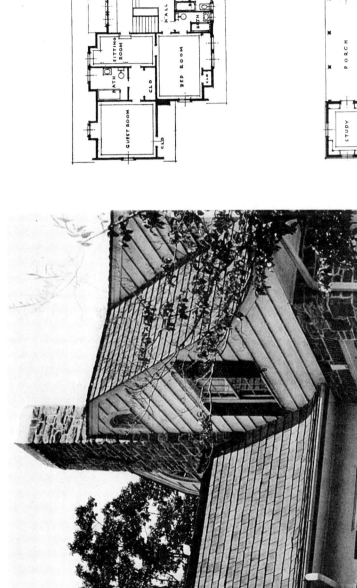

DETAIL OF END—RESIDENCE OF B. F. WINCHELL, JR., ON FIELDSTON RD., UPPER N. Y. C.

DWIGHT JAMES BAUM, ARCHITECT, NEW YORK

SECOND FLOOR PLAN

FIRST FLOOR PLAN

RESIDENCE OF MR. FRANK ROLLINS, FIELDSTON, N. Y.

DWIGHT JAMES BAUM, ARCHITECT, NEW YORK

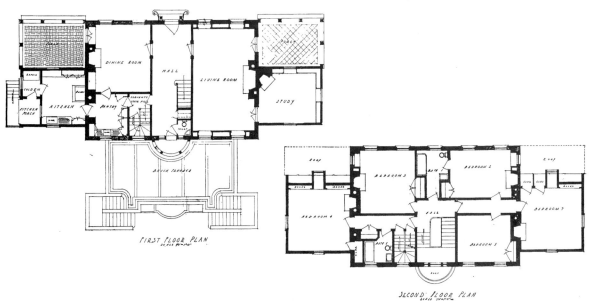

FIRST FLOOR PLAN

SECOND FLOOR PLAN

GENERAL VIEW—RESIDENCE OF DR. LYNN FULKERSON, FIELDSTON, N. Y.
DWIGHT JAMES BAUM, ARCHITECT, NEW YORK

VIEW ON TERRACE OVER GARAGE

DETAIL OF MAIN ENTRANCE

RESIDENCE OF DR. LYNN FULKERSON, FIELDSTON, N. Y.

DWIGHT JAMES BAUM, ARCHITECT, NEW YORK

26

DETAIL OF STUDY MANTEL

RESIDENCE OF DR. LYNN FULKERSON, FIELDSTON, N. Y.

DETAIL OF INTERIOR DOORS IN LIVING ROOM

DWIGHT JAMES BAUM, ARCHITECT, NEW YORK

27

RESIDENCE OF MR. ROBERT FEIN OPPOSITE VAN CORTLANDT PARK, NEW YORK CITY
DWIGHT JAMES BAUM, ARCHITECT, NEW YORK

DETAIL OF MAIN ENTRANCE—RESIDENCE OF MR. ROBERT FEIN

29

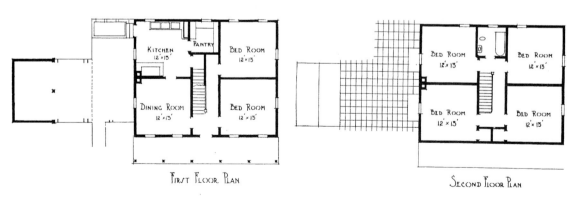

First Floor Plan

Second Floor Plan

SUP'T COTTAGE, ESTATE OF GLENN STEWART, ESQ., LOCUST VALLEY, L. I.
ALFRED HOPKINS, ARCHITECT, NEW YORK

SECOND FLOOR PLAN.

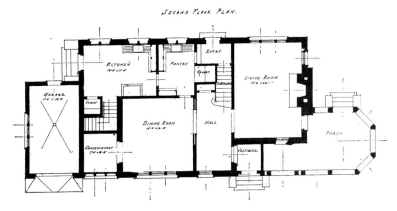

HOUSE AT FOREST HILLS, L. I.

SAGE FOUNDATION COMPANY, ARCHITECTS, NEW YORK

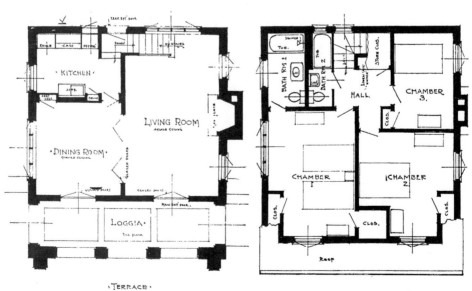

HOUSE OF JAMES ROY ALLEN, ARCHITECT, CHICAGO, ILL.

SECOND · FLOOR · PLAN ·

FIRST FLOOR PLAN ·

HOUSE FOR MRS. S. S. CARLETON, BRONXVILLE, N. Y.

ALFRED BUSSELLE, ARCHITECT, NEW YORK

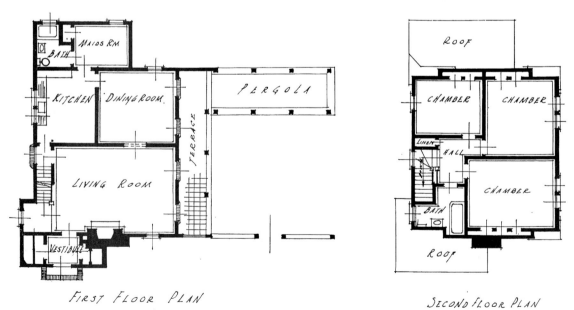

FIRST FLOOR PLAN
SCALE 1/8"=1'-0"

SECOND FLOOR PLAN
SCALE 1/8"=1'-0"

RESIDENCE FOR J. E. SAMPLE, ESQ., HOWELL PARK, LARCHMONT, N. Y.
C. A. PATTERSON, ARCHITECT, NEW YORK

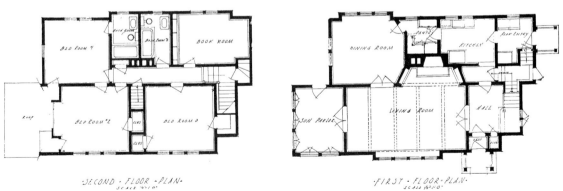

SECOND · FLOOR · PLAN·

FIRST · FLOOR · PLAN·

RESIDENCE FOR EDWARD ROCK, ESQ., FOREST HEIGHTS, NEW ROCHELLE, N. Y.
GEO. A. LICHT, ARCHITECT, NEW YORK

RESIDENCE OF MR. DWIGHT JAMES BAUM, ARCHITECT, FIELDSTON, N. Y.

36

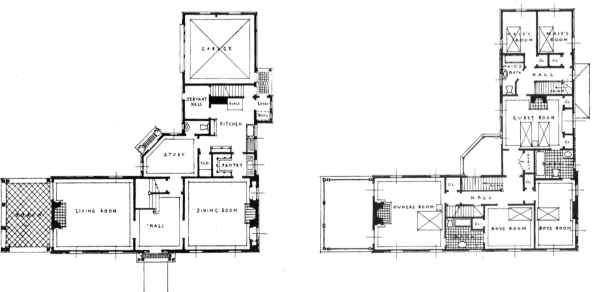

MAIN ENTRANCE—RESIDENCE OF DWIGHT JAMES BAUM, ARCHITECT, AT FIELDSTON, N. Y.

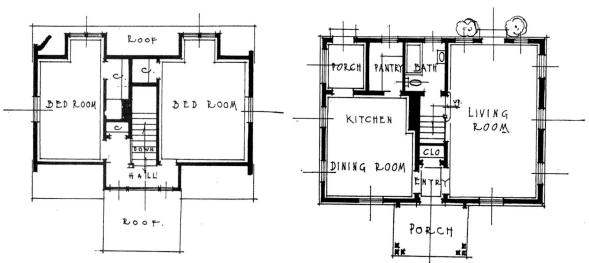

COTTAGE ON ESTATE OF PRENTICE S ANGER, ESQ., LAKE SIENAPIE, N. H.
PRENTICE SANGER, ARCHITECT, NEW YORK

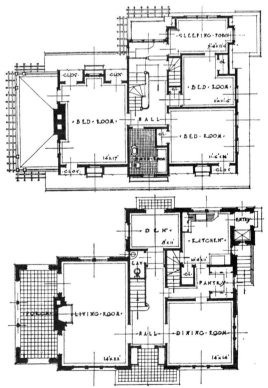

HOUSE FOR H. M. GREEN, ESQ., KEW GARDENS, L. I.

WALTER McQUADE, ARCHITECT, NEW YORK

RESIDENCE FOR MR. GEO. R. AINSWORTH, KENSINGTON, GREAT NECK, L. I.
AYMAR EMBURY II, ARCHITECT, NEW YORK

FIRST · FLOOR · PLAN ·

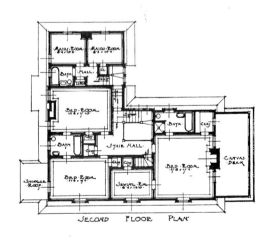

SECOND · FLOOR · PLAN ·

COTTAGE FOR MRS. E. L. BUSHNELL, GARDEN CITY, L. I.

AYMAR EMBURY II, ARCHITECT, NEW YORK

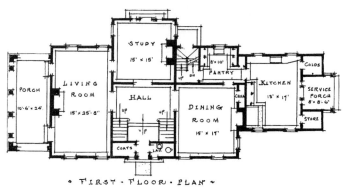

· FIRST · FLOOR · PLAN ·

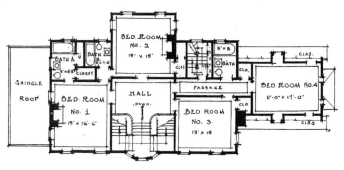

· SECOND · FLOOR · PLAN ·

HOUSE OF MRS. I. F. WARDWELL, STAMFORD, CONN.

AYMAR EMBURY II, ARCHITECT, NEW YORK

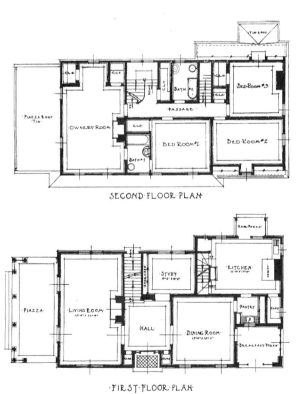

SECOND·FLOOR·PLAN

FIRST·FLOOR·PLAN

HOUSE OF MRS. GEORGE M. GALES—KENSINGTON, GREAT NECK, L. I.

AYMAR EMBURY II, ARCHITECT, NEW YORK

C. A. PATTERSON, ARCHITECT, NEW YORK

RESIDENCE FOR PAUL SHIELDS, ESQ., GREAT NECK, L. I.

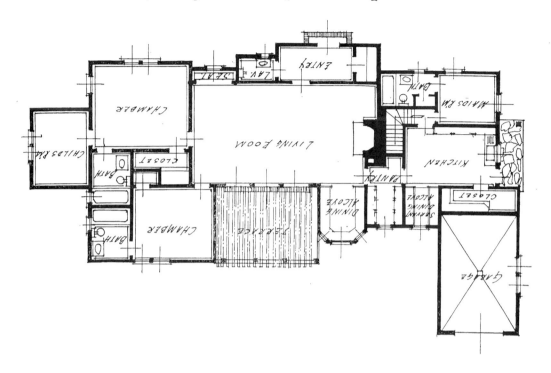

FIRST FLOOR PLAN
SCALE 1/8" = ONE FT

PAUL SHIELDS RESIDENCE, GREAT NECK, L. I.

45

RESIDENCE OF ARNO KOLBE, ESQ., PARK HILL, YONKERS, N. Y.

ARNO KOLBE, ARCHITECT, NEW YORK

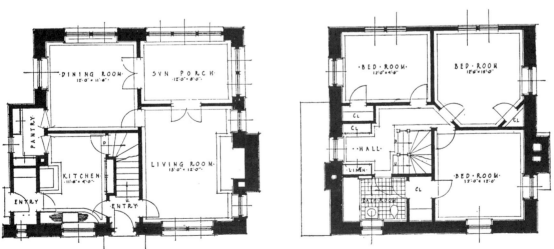

HOUSE FOR B. A. BENEDICT, ESQ., LARCHMONT, N. Y.

JULIUS GREGORY, ARCHITECT, NEW YORK

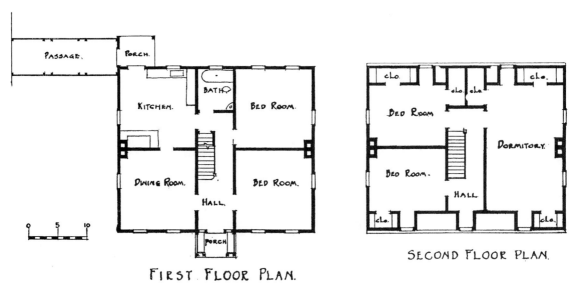

FIRST FLOOR PLAN.

SECOND FLOOR PLAN.

HOUSE FOR MR. ADOLF MOLLENHAUER, BAYSHORE, L. I.

ALFRED HOPKINS, ARCHITECT, NEW YORK

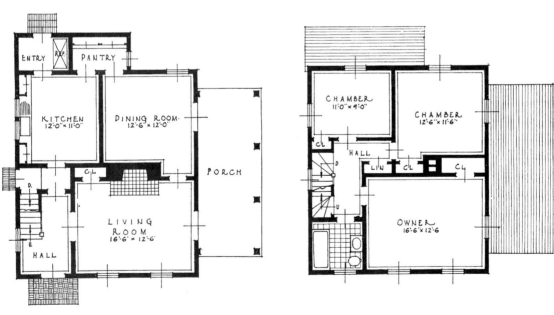

FIRST FLOOR PLAN   SECOND FLOOR PLAN

HOUSE FOR MR. EUGENE KRUSKAL, PELHAM MANOR, N. Y.

JULIUS GREGORY, ARCHITECT, NEW YORK

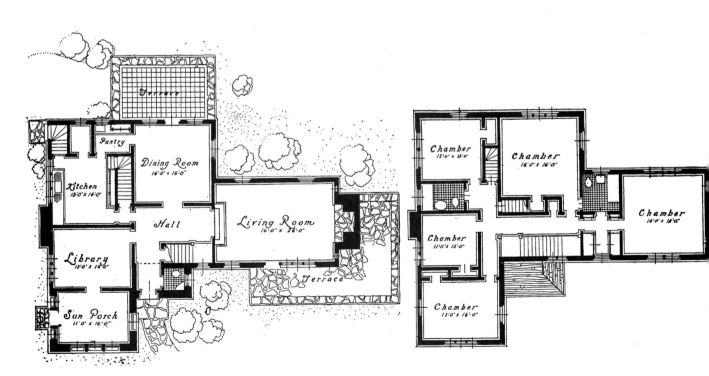

HOUSE OF MR. CLARENCE McDANIEL, HARTSDALE, N. Y.

JULIUS GREGORY, ARCHITECT, NEW YORK

50

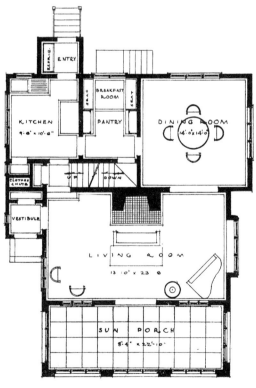

FIRST FLOOR PLAN

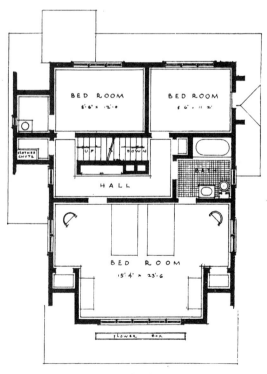

SECOND FLOOR PLAN

HOUSE AT KEW GARDENS

WM. E. HAUGAARD, ARCHITECT, NEW YORK

51

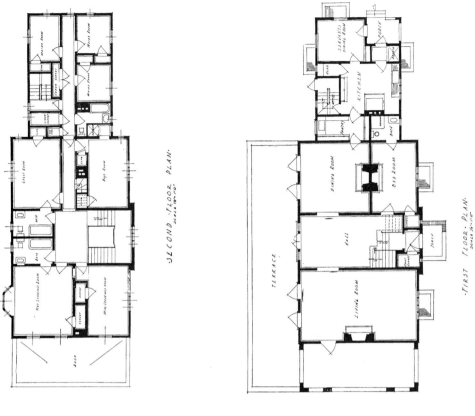

SECOND FLOOR PLAN

FIRST FLOOR PLAN

HOUSE FOR MRS. LAURA LEVERING, GREENWICH, CONN.

PHELPS BARNUM, BERNARD W. CLOSE, ASSOCIATED ARCHITECTS

HOUSE FOR MRS. LAURA LEVERING

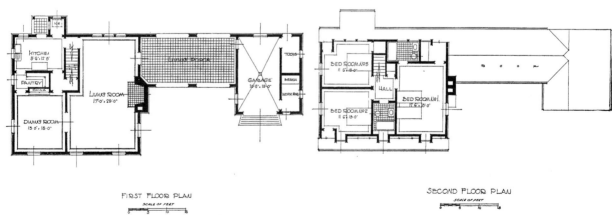

FIRST FLOOR PLAN
SCALE OF FEET

SECOND FLOOR PLAN
SCALE OF FEET

HOUSE OF MR. ROBERT MEARS, JR., TENAFLY, N. J.
R. C. HUNTER AND BRO., ARCHITECTS, NEW YORK

LITTLE ORCHARD FARM, WHITE PLAINS, N. Y.

FRANK J. FORSTER, ARCHITECT, NEW YORK

55

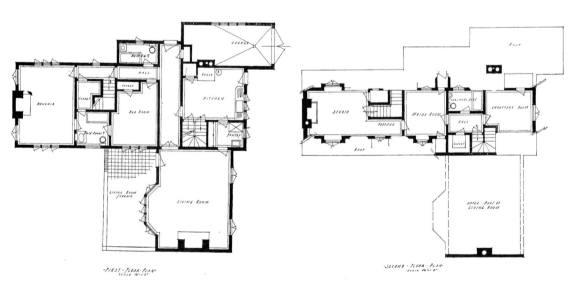

LITTLE ORCHARD FARM

GARDENER'S COTTAGE, LATHROP BROWN, ST. JAMES, L. I.

PEABODY, WILSON AND BROWN, ARCHITECTS, NEW YORK

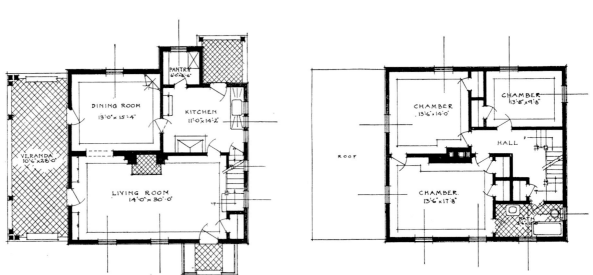

RESIDENCE FOR FRANCIS E. FALKENBURG, ESQ., BRONXVILLE, N. Y.

FRANK J. FORSTER, ARCHITECT, NEW YORK

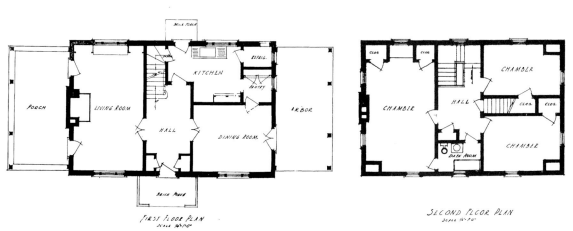

FIRST FLOOR PLAN
SCALE ¼"=1'0"

SECOND FLOOR PLAN
SCALE ¼"=1'0"

HOUSE OF GORDON STEWART, ESQ.

FRANK J. FORSTER, ARCHITECT, NEW YORK

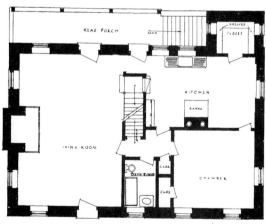

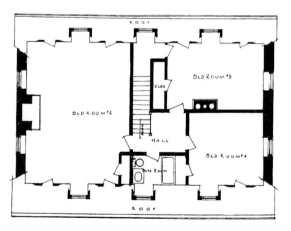

FIRST FLOOR PLAN
SCALE ¼"=1'-0"

SECOND FLOOR PLAN
SCALE ¼"=1'-0"

COTTAGE FOR R. HALLADAY, DEMAREST, N. J.

FRANK J. FORSTER, ARCHITECT, NEW YORK

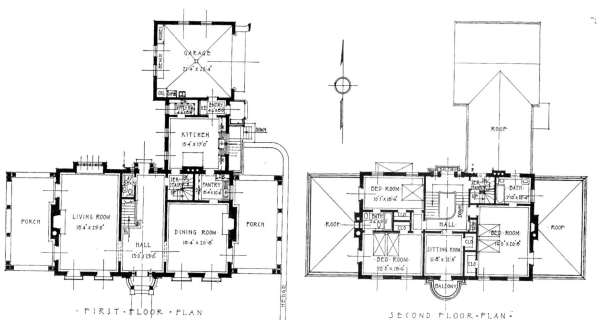

HOUSE FOR MR. HENRY R. SWARTLEY, JR., GREAT NECK, L. I.

BATES AND HOW, ARCHITECTS, NEW YORK

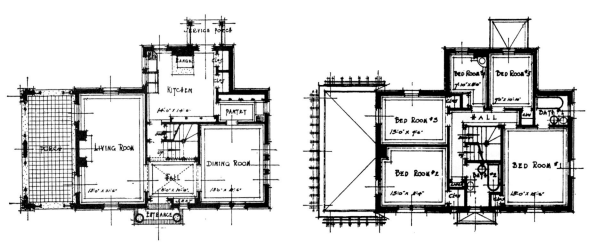

RESIDENCE AT GREAT NECK, L. I.

AYMAR EMBURY II, ARCHITECT, NEW YORK

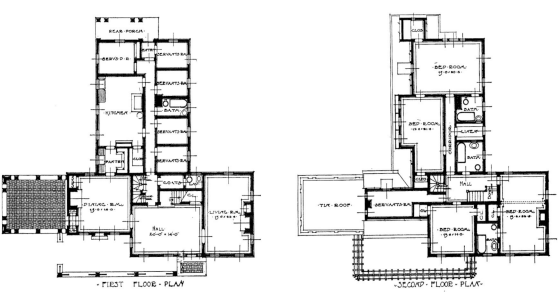

RESIDENCE OF MR. MARSHAL FRY, SOUTHAMPTON, L. I.

AYMAR EMBURY II, ARCHITECT, NEW YORK

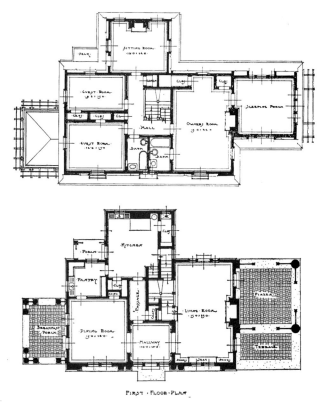

FIRST · FLOOR · PLAN

HOUSE FOR MR. F. C. NOBLE, NEW CANAAN, CONN.

AYMAR EMBURY II, ARCHITECT, NEW YORK

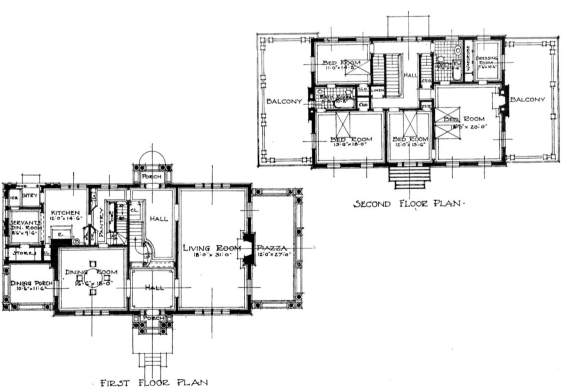

SECOND FLOOR PLAN.

FIRST FLOOR PLAN

HOUSE FOR MR. W. W. ELZEA, SAGAMORE, BRONXVILLE, N. Y.

BATES AND HOW, ARCHITECTS, NEW YORK

PLAN OF SECOND FLOOR

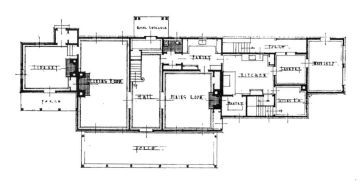

PLAN OF FIRST FLOOR

HOUSE FOR MR. JAMES S. COBB, PAWLIN, L. I.

ALFRED BUSSELLE, ARCHITECT, NEW YORK

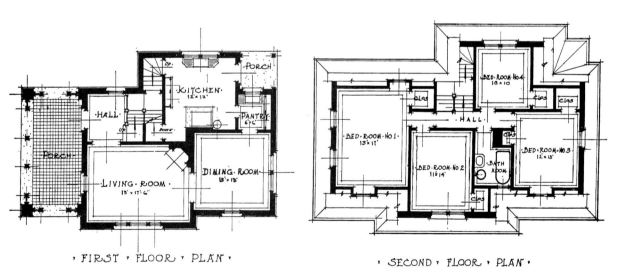

· FIRST · FLOOR · PLAN ·

· SECOND · FLOOR · PLAN ·

HOUSE AT FOREST HILLS

AYMAR EMBURY II, ARCHITECT, NEW YORK

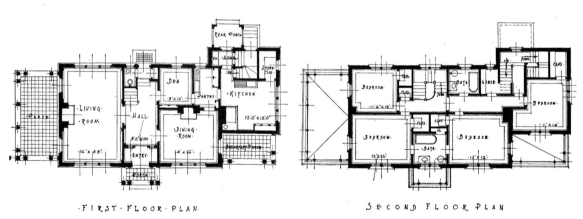

·FIRST·FLOOR·PLAN·   SECOND FLOOR PLAN

HOUSE AT GARDEN CITY, L. I.

ALFRED BUSSELLE, ARCHITECT, NEW YORK

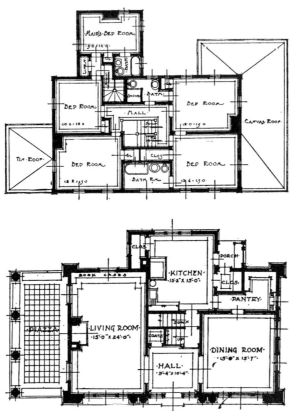

HOUSE FOR F. P. CLARKE, ESQ., GARDEN CITY, L. I.

AYMAR EMBURY II, ARCHITECT, NEW YORK

RESIDENCE OF MR. D. W. NYE, KEW, L. I.

AYMAR EMBURY II, ARCHITECT, NEW YORK

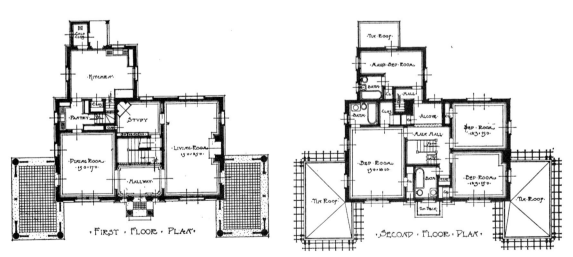

RESIDENCE OF MR. GEO. M. TAYLOR, MILBURN, N. J.

AYMAR EMBURY II, ARCHITECT, NEW YORK

RESIDENCE FOR MR. R. M. ELLIS AT KENSINGTON, GREAT NECK, L. I.

AYMAR EMBURY II, ARCHITECT, NEW YORK

COUNTRY AND SUBURBAN HOUSES OF THE TWENTIES

HOUSE FOR C. O. BARING, ESQ., HARTSDALE, N. Y.

FRANK J. FORSTER, ARCHITECT, NEW YORK

73

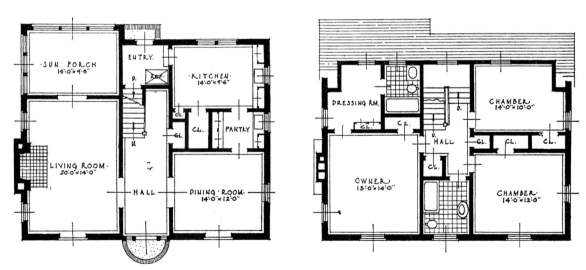

HOUSE FOR MR. CHARLES KIELY, PELHAM MANOR, N. Y.

JULIUS GREGORY, ARCHITECT, NEW YORK

HOUSE BY JULIUS GREGORY, ARCHITECT, N. Y.

R. C. HUNTER AND BRO., ARCHITECTS, NEW YORK

HOUSE OF SHELDON S. YATES, ESQ., ENGLEWOOD, N. J.

76

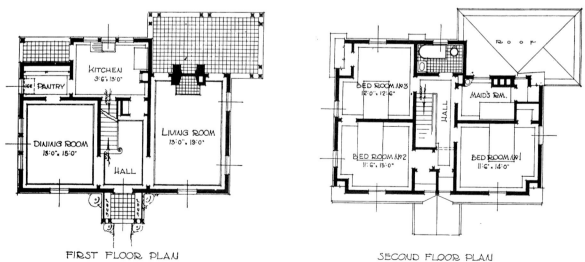

FIRST FLOOR PLAN

SECOND FLOOR PLAN

HOUSE OF SHELDON S. YATES, ESQ., ENGLEWOOD, N. J.

R. C. HUNTER AND BRO., ARCHITECTS, NEW YORK

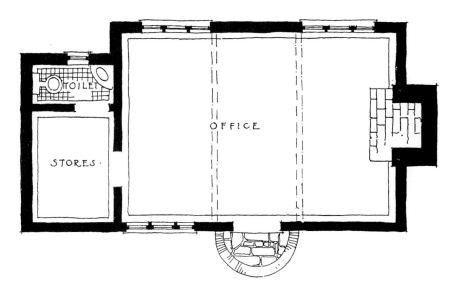

OFFICE FOR HARVEY CRAW, ESQ., GREAT NECK, L. I.

FRANK J. FORSTER, ARCHITECT, NEW YORK

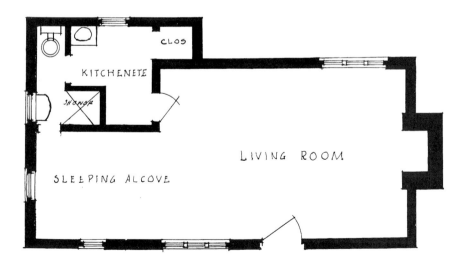

STUDIO FOR JACK SHERIDAN, ESQ., PORT WASHINGTON, L. I.

FRANK J. FORSTER, ARCHITECT, NEW YORK

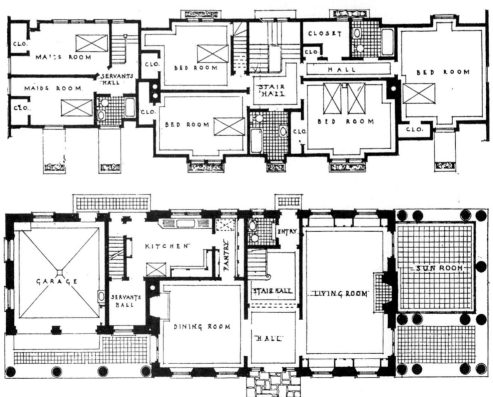

RESIDENCE OF MR. CHAS. EVANS ON WEST 250TH ST., UPPER NEW YORK CITY
DWIGHT JAMES BAUM, ARCHITECT, NEW YORK

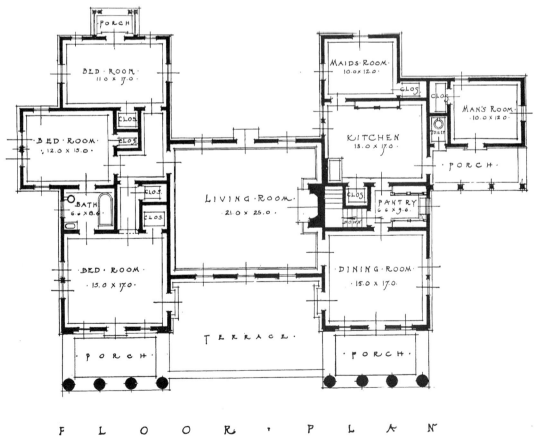

F L O O R · P L A N

BUNGALOW FOR MR. ST. GEORGE BARBER, SOUTH RIVER, MARYLAND

AYMAR EMBURY II, ARCHITECT, NEW YORK

GARAGE FOR REG. HALLADAY, ESQ., ENGLEWOOD, N. J.

FRANK J. FORSTER, ARCHITECT, NEW YORK

82

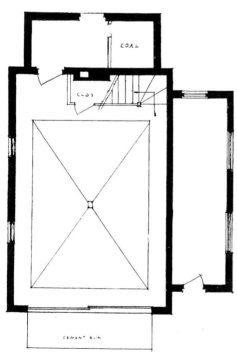

GARAGE FLOOR PLAN

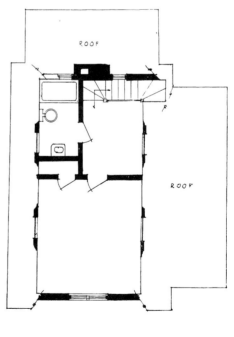

SECOND FLOOR PLAN

GARAGE OF JOHN B. VAN HALLEN, ESQ., HARTSDALE, N. Y.

FRANK J. FORSTER, ARCHITECT, NEW YORK

FRONT ELEVATION—RESIDENCE FOR W. T. JEFFERSON, ESQ., PASADENA, CAL.

MARSTON AND VAN PELT, ARCHITECTS, PASADENA

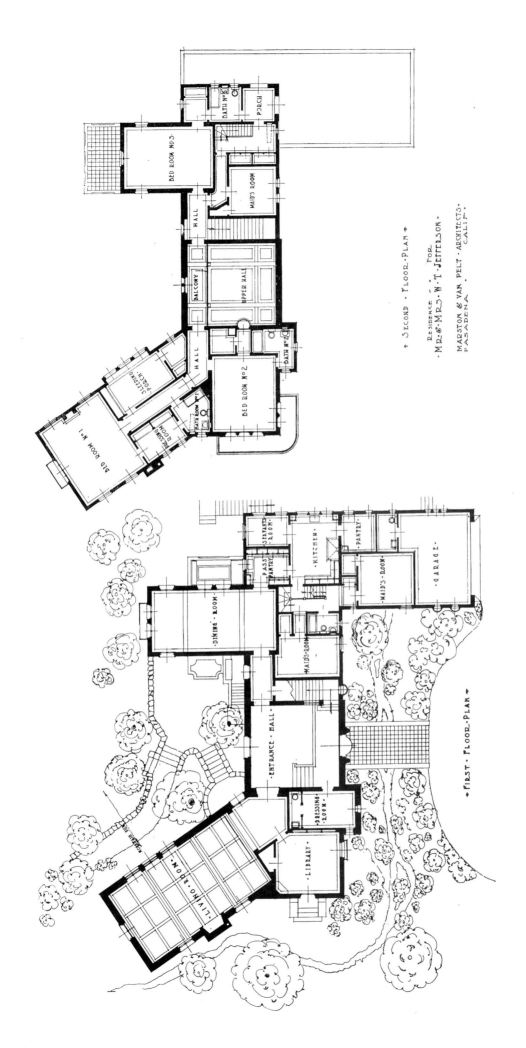

+ SECOND · FLOOR · PLAN +

RESIDENCE · · · FOR
MR · & · MRS · W · T · JEFFERSON ·

MARSTON & VAN PELT · ARCHITECTS ·
PASADENA · CALIF ·

BED ROOM NO.3

BATH NO.3

PORCH

MAID'S ROOM

HALL

BALCONY

UPPER HALL

SLEEPING PORCH

HALL

BATH NO.2

BED ROOM NO.1

BATH ROOM NO.1

DRESSING ROOM

BED ROOM NO.2

SERVANTS ROOM

PASS PANTRY

KITCHEN

PANTRY

DINING · ROOM

MAID'S · ROOM

MAID'S ROOM

GARAGE ·

ENTRANCE · HALL ·

DRESSING · ROOM ·

LIBRARY ·

LIVING · ROOM ·

+ FIRST · FLOOR · PLAN +

85

COUNTRY AND SUBURBAN HOUSES OF THE TWENTIES

STAIRWAY—JEFFERSON RESIDENCE, PASADENA

STREET ENTRANCE—W. T. JEFFERSON RESIDENCE, PASADENA

86

RESIDENCE FOR MR. SETH W. P. STRELINGEN, BEVERLY HILLS, CAL.

H. H. WHITELEY, ARCHITECT, LOS ANGELES, CAL.

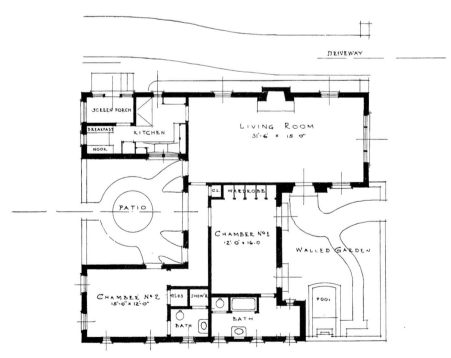

HOUSE FOR MR. SETH W. P. STRELINGEN, BEVERLY HILLS, CAL.
H. H. WHITELEY, ARCHITECT, LOS ANGELES, CAL.

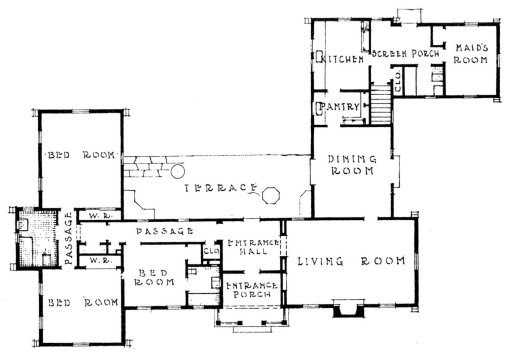

FLOOR. PLAN

HOUSE FOR MR. BRIGGS C. KECK, PASADENA, CAL.

REGINALD D. JOHNSON, ARCHITECT, PASADENA

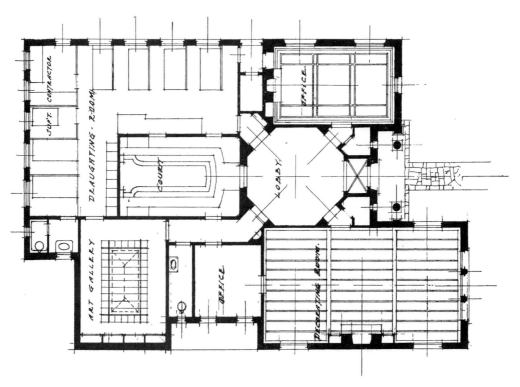

STUDIO OF MR. H. H. WHITELEY, LOS ANGELES, CAL.—DESIGNED BY HIMSELF

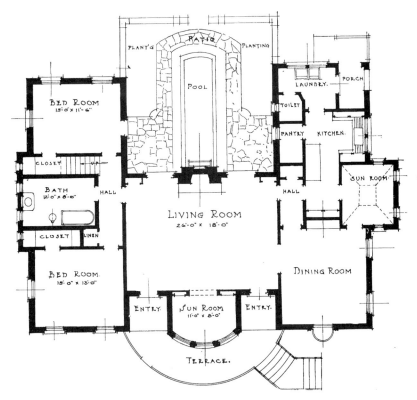

A HOUSE BY H. H. WHITELEY, ARCHITECT, LOS ANGELES, CAL.

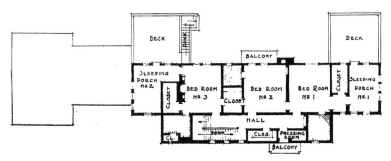

PLAN OF SECOND FLOOR

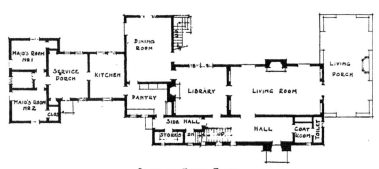

PLAN OF FIRST FLOOR

HOUSE FOR MR. C. F. PAXTON, PASADENA, CAL.

REGINALD D. JOHNSON, ARCHITECT, PASADENA

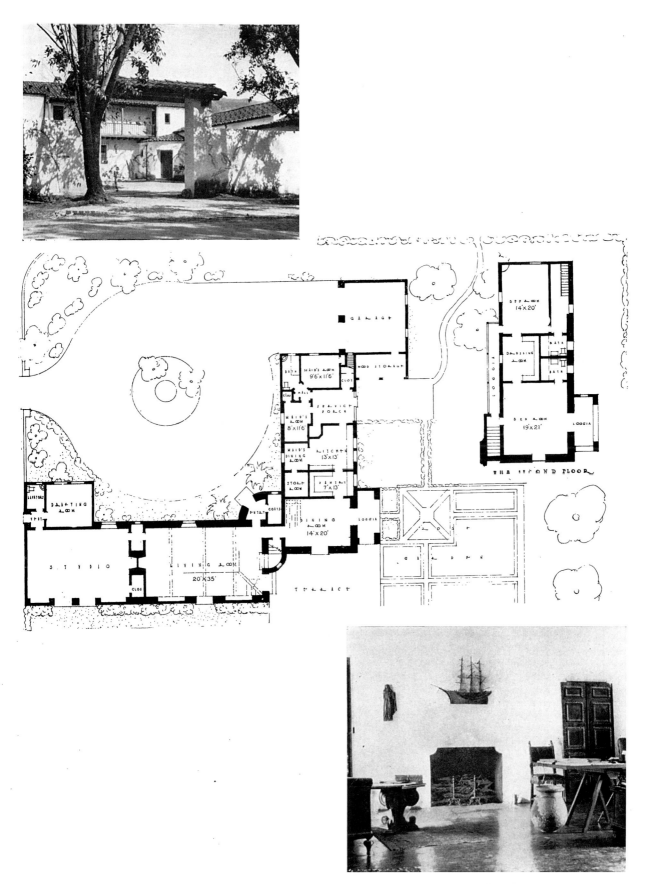

RESIDENCE OF GEORGE WASHINGTON SMITH, ARCHITECT, SANTA BARBARA, CAL.

ENTRANCE PATIO GEORGE WASHINGTON SMITH RESIDENCE, SANTA BARBARA, CAL.

RESIDENCE OF CRAIG HEBERTON, ESQ., SANTA BARBARA
GEO. WASHINGTON SMITH, ARCHITECT, SANTA BARBARA, CAL.

GARAGE ENTRANCE

ENTRANCE

CRAIG HEBERTON RESIDENCE, SANTA BARBARA, CAL.

GEO. WASHINGTON SMITH, ARCHITECT, SANTA BARBARA, CAL.

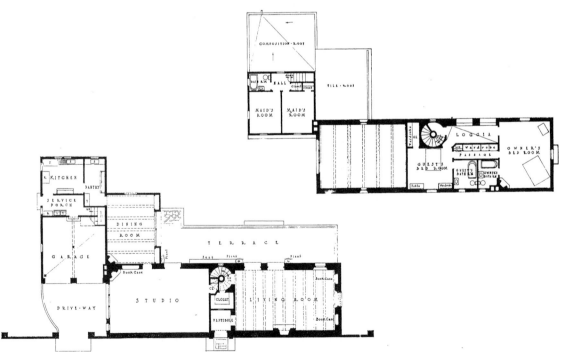

FIRST FLOOR PLAN

CRAIG HEBERTON RESIDENCE, SANTA BARBARA, CAL.

RESIDENCE FOR MR. H. L. BRAINARD, SANTA BARBARA, CAL.
GEO. WASHINGTON SMITH, ARCHITECT, SANTA BARBARA, CAL.

STUDIO—BRAINARD RESIDENCE, SANTA BARBARA

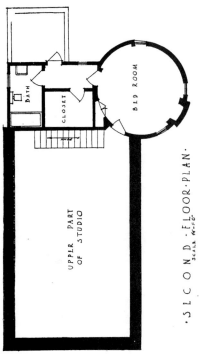

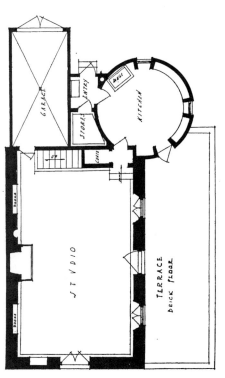

FLOOR PLANS OF BRAINARD RESIDENCE

RESIDENCE FOR MR. C. C. STANLEY, PASADENA

MARSTON AND VAN PELT, ARCHITECTS, PASADENA

GARDEN ENTRANCE JOHN HENRY MEYER RESIDENCE, SAN MARINO, CAL.

MARSTON AND VAN PELT, ARCHITECTS, PASADENA

~ SECOND · FLOOR · PLAN ~

RESIDENCE FOR
~ MR · JOHN · H · MEYER ~

MARSTON & VAN PELT · ARCHITECTS ·
PASADENA   CALIFORNIA

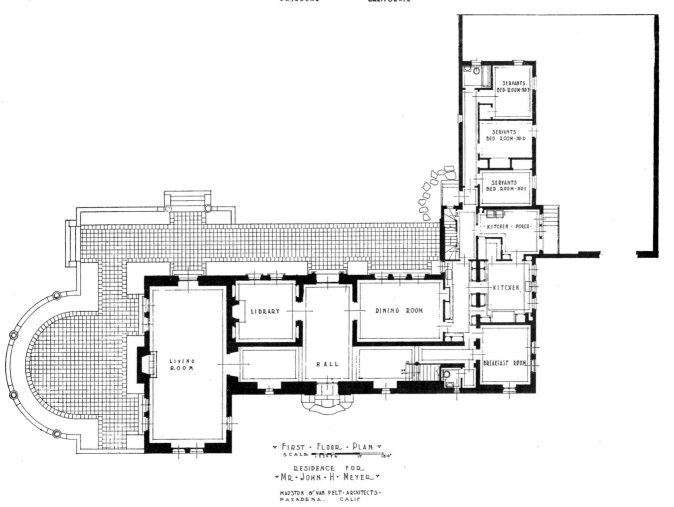

~ FIRST · FLOOR · PLAN ~

SCALE

RESIDENCE FOR
~ MR · JOHN · H · MEYER ~

MARSTON & VAN PELT · ARCHITECTS ·
PASADENA. CALIF

TERRACE—RESIDENCE OF JOHN HENRY MEYER, ESQ., SAN MARINO, CAL.
MARSTON AND VAN PELT, ARCHITECTS, PASADENA

ENTRANCE DETAIL—JOHN HENRY MEYER RESIDENCE, SAN MARINO, CAL.

SECOND STORY HALL—JOHN HENRY MEYER RESIDENCE